ROAD MAP TO YOUR JOB

Navigating to Each Pit Stop on the Road to Employment

By Trevor Morgan

Copyright © 2018 by Trevor Morgan

CONTENTS

ABOUT THE AUTHOR

 **T**revor Morgan had a 2.64 GPA during his freshman year of college, and he was pursuing a degree in agribusiness. Just one year later, he earned a business management internship at a Fortune 200 aerospace engineering company. He currently works full-time at that same company in a business management role, and he has also been fortunate to gain experience in a supply chain management role during his time at the company. As a young professional, he has benefited from a fully company-funded Master's level education at Northwestern University, and he has well-surpassed his own expectations so far in his career.

Through self-reflection, Trevor has recognized his fortunate experiences as well as the numerous, valuable insights that job seekers facing similar challenges can learn and apply from his story. As the author of this book, Trevor provides the keys to overcoming qualification barriers in your job or internship search.

$$\Delta \Delta \Delta$$

Trevor's key experiences that led to the insights he provides throughout the book are summarized below.

Trevor:

Found His Network

After struggling through career fairs and receiving several job application rejection emails, Trevor used his network to obtain an internship at a Fortune 200 aerospace-engineering company.

Trevor would eventually obtain and accept a full-time position at the same company after interning for two summers during his college career. In his recent reflections, Trevor has realized the importance of building a strong network before and during any job search.

Sharpened His Story

About half way through his freshman year of college, Trevor began to reflect on his background, strengths, and weaknesses.

Trevor had previously focused more on job descriptions and qualifications as opposed to his own background, strengths, and weaknesses. His best interviews came after he habitually reflected on his own background.

Creatively Presented His Story

Trevor began to creatively present his skill set and experiences on his résumé, website, and elsewhere. Not only did this practice make Trevor's job search more enjoyable, but it also strengthened his ability to identify key skills, strengths, and his plans to overcome his weaknesses.

Grew Confidence in Communicating His Story

As he progressed through school, Trevor learned to habitually think through and explain his skill set to others. His ability to confidently communicate the application of his growing skill set grew, and he obtained numerous interviews.

Succeeded in Interviews and Received Numerous Offers

After utilizing key resources to learn how to interview, practicing his learnings, and preparing for each interview, Trevor found success in his interviews. He received three full-time job offers near the end of his senior year, all of which he found intriguing.

READ THIS FIRST

This book serves as a handbook to any job or internship seeker. Each of the Five Pit Stops in this book starts with the definition and importance of the Pit Stop. Subsequently, I provide an actionable framework of steps, or Road Map, to practice for that section. After the Road Map in each Pit Stop, I provide further detail, example experiences, and the main takeaways of the Pit Stop. While I recommend reading and practicing each Pit Stop in its entirety, this book is also useful for quick reference.

Find the general format for each Pit Stop directly below:

- Pit Stop Definition
- Reason Pit Stop is Important
- Steps to Complete for Pit Stop
- More Details on Why
- My Personal Experience and Insights
- Tips, Tricks, and Inspiration from My Road Trip

△△△

Here are some important terms to reference as needed during your reading:

Job- Any task, internship, career, or role that requires screening before you can do it. While I use the word "Job" throughout this book, the practices described in the book are applicable any time a person is trying to stand out to obtain a role or position.

Potential Hirer/ Hiring Manager- Any person influencing the likelihood that you receive an offer for a role or position. These people could be recruiters, actual managers of a department within a company, or any other person with influence over your ability to obtain a role or position. Throughout this book, I use the words "potential hirer" and "hiring manager" in an effort to cover the broad variety of people with influence over your job application.

△△△

I provide many other definitions, references, and various tools in the appendix of this book.

INTRODUCTION
WHY I WROTE THIS BOOK

I started struggling for breath as I scrolled through my university's career site grasping for any possible job opportunities. My mind was racing. How did I feel so bad when I felt like I put in more time and effort studying and working on my résumé than most other students? I thought to myself "Am I hungover? I only had a few beers last night... that doesn't seem right." So how come all of these jobs listed basic qualifications that I didn't meet? Did I really have to have a 3.6 GPA in the School of Business to be qualified to do entry level work? I knew I could do most of these jobs. After all, I was a quick learner and a hard worker. My confidence didn't make me feel any better at that moment, though.

Almost a decade later, I sit here and realize that many college students, recent graduates, or professionals who are trying to start a career with a low GPA *perceive* substantial obstacles in trying to obtain their job of choice. In their mind, they often have the "wrong" degree, insufficient relevant experience, an unacceptable GPA, or various other weaknesses that they try to mask and that they fail to mitigate during their job search process. Why are so many job seekers perceiving these insurmountable obstacles during their job search?

Publicly available recruiting and job posting sites, career fairs and centers, university lectures, competitive peers, and other job search resources are all screaming "you **HAVE** to meet the minimum qualifications." Minimum qualifications are listed on every job posting and are often embedded in a recruiter's screening process, causing them to filter out applications instantly. Job seekers quickly become discouraged as they receive rejection email after rejection email, which are typically automated, providing no real feedback other than "other candidates were more closely qualified for this position." In an attempt to conceal their perceived lack of qualifications, discouraged job seekers typically ramble about their successes when they talk to career fair booth recruiters or even when they talk to their peers. While it is worthwhile for a job seeker to know and to be able to talk about their strengths, and while it is notable that discouraged job seekers still make an attempt at career fairs or through other outlets, it is more notable that they are often not having a real, two-sided conversation with the person listening. Unfortunately, most of these discouraged job seekers eventually run out of time, motivation, or other resources such as money, and they settle for an average, potential-limiting job.

If someone has told you that you "have to meet the minimum qualifications," they were lying to you. You don't have to meet the minimum qualifications. Minimum qualifications are often just nice to have, but not mandatory for the role. If you can do the work as well as anyone else, you can (and should) be hired to do the work. You have to show the potential hirer that they can trust you to do the work for which they are hiring. While many companies do have written minimum qualifications, a hiring manager typically determines the minimum qualifications, so they can often adjust listed qualifications or omit qualifications from the listing. Even if the qualifications are firm requirements from a company's Human Resources department, the company typically will have processes in place so that a hiring manager can request that the human resources department make an exception to the listed qualifications. While I am not saying that you can take shortcuts and fail a bunch of classes or skip college and still get your job of choice, I *am* saying that there are many ways outside of the standard job search sites and standard recruiting channels to stand out. If you have been discouraged in your job pursuits, or if you would just like a helpful guide to assist in your job search, this book will serve as your catalyst.

By virtue of reading this book, deep down, you respect yourself and know that you deserve the job of your choice. You know that you either hold skills that could create value for a company, or that you are at least willing to put in the time and hard work to learn and develop those skills. Whatever your situation is, you face perceived obstacles to obtaining the job that you want, but deep down you know these obstacles are surmountable.

$$\triangle \triangle \triangle$$

Welcome to the Road Map to Your Job.

PIT STOP #1: BUILDING YOUR SOUND NETWORK

Meeting Potential Hosts for Your Road Trip

BUILDING YOUR SOUND NETWORK

YOU HAVE TO FIND SOMEONE WHO IS WILLING TO HOST YOU IN ORDER FOR YOUR ROAD TRIP TO HAVE A DESTINATION

We start our journey with Pit Stop #1- Building Your Sound Network. Building Your Sound Network is the process of getting to truly know people, what they do, what their skills and challenges are, and relating your background to their daily lives. Ultimately, you will use the knowledge you gain during this Pit Stop to determine which job you consider the destination of your metaphorical road trip.

NETWORK TO START THE CONVERSATION

When you are planning a road trip, you determine your destination. You might determine your destination mid-road trip, or you might decide on your destination well before the road trip. Either way, you consider factors such as location, weather, day-to-day activities, restaurants, night life, and others in order to make your decision, and you often learn even more about your destination on your way to it. Similarly, job seekers consider factors such as company culture, salary, work-life balance, work requirements and activities, as well as others to determine if the company and role appeal to them. Networking enables a job seeker to become more knowledgable and more prepared for a potential interview, providing immediate benefit even if the job seeker already knows a certain job is their dream job.

On the other hand, just like a friend or an AirBnB host has to be willing to host a road tripper, an employer has to be willing to offer a job seeker a role at their company. In other words, getting hired for your dream job is a two-way street. Networking enables the interested job seeker to learn more about the job to further assess their interests, and it allows an employer to build a trusting relationship with a potential employee.

$$\triangle\triangle\triangle$$

Once you have consistently implemented your learnings from this Pit Stop, you will be able to build a trusting relationship with your potential hirer.

ROAD MAP TO MEETING POTENTIAL HOSTS

So how are you going to build your sound network?

ΔΔΔ

Here is the simple process:

1) Recognize your daily opportunity to build a network

Every person has a daily routine in which there are many opportunities to learn about and/or meet and get to know a potential hirer.

To recognize your daily opportunity to network:

1a) Reflect on and list any and all activities you do each day of the week or month (just get them written down or typed, format is irrelevant)

What tasks do you do, or could you do, daily or weekly that involve other people or that are at least somewhere where other people are present?

Common tasks include: attending class, attending happy hour, going to the gym, going to the pool, studying at the library, going to a club meeting, going to a career fair, practicing or playing a sport, going to a university sponsored lecture, and many more.

1b) Next to each of your listed activities, mark an "X" if you normally interact with people during the activity

If you don't have at least 3 "X"s," mark "X"s next to the 3 activities during which you are most able to interact with others. Make note that you will purposely interact with others the next time you do one of these activities.

1c) Write down 1-3 people that you might interact with during the activity that might have any knowledge about a specific company and/or role

Common people include: students or other peers, professors, coaches, teaching assistants, friends, friend's parents or a peer's parents, recruiters, your own parents, your parents' friends or peers, and many more.

1d) Lastly, write down names or descriptions of contacts that each of the people you listed above might know or interact with who might have knowledge about a specific industry, company, or even a specific role of your interest

While this seems like a stretch, you will be surprised at the possibilities you activate when you realize your 2nd and 3rd level connections.

Just like the social media platform LinkedIn, in real life you often are one connection away from a potential hirer. Using LinkedIn can also enable you to start a connection with your potential hirer, one that you can build upon in-person.

$$\triangle\triangle\triangle$$

After you have made your first attempt at the above steps, you have completed the rough draft of your network. By completing this step, you have made your network physically visible, enabling you to more easily realize the connections you can make during your normal activities. Therefore, you have already taken your first step closer to your dream job, and you have momentum on your side.

Now that you have your rough draft network, move to step two and keep your draft handy so that you can reference and update it as needed.

2) With your network draft in mind, build true relationships with the most relevant (to your known career interests) network connections identified in your draft network

2a) While going through your day-to day activities, converse with the most relevant people you have identified in your draft network, and try to really get to know their background (example questions provided below)

- What do they do?

- Where are they from?
- What did they study and where?
- What are their strengths?
- What are their weaknesses?
- What are their hobbies?
- Other questions that help you understand their background and lifestyle

If you happen to know a connection is in or knows someone in an industry, company, or role of your interest, be sure to focus more of your time and energy building that relationship.

Note: You might have to go out of your comfort zone to meet or interact with some of the relevant people you listed in your draft network. Even if the relevant connection is a friend of a friend of one of your peers, most people are willing to at least talk via email with someone who is seeking a mentor or someone who is just looking to learn for career purposes.

ΔΔΔ

Learning about a person's life will open the door for you, even if it's only on a subconscious level, to begin connecting your background to their background. Getting to know them will enable you to relate to them and build a true relationship, which will exponentially increase the likelihood

17

that they will take positive action to increase your chances of getting hired or even take action to hire you themselves. From their perspective, as you converse and relate, they will find familiarity in you, and at the very least, subconsciously connect with that familiarity (at some point they were likely asking the same questions or at least trying to learn the same information earlier in their careers). This process of relating your background to theirs will also help you to start to understand how your background will be useful at the company, or within the role of your interest. We will dive deeper into this valuable process in Pit Stop #2- Sharpening Your Story.

3) Lastly, learn about that person's day-to-day work

Getting to know what they do each day and what challenges they face will help you understand how your background can be applied to the job as well as whether you are even interested in the job.

Whether you realize it or not, in getting to know someone and their day-to-day activities, you are already prepping for a potential interview, separating yourself from other potential candidates, and weeding out opportunities that you don't like.

3a) Ask questions to learn about their day-to-day work

Below are example questions you might use:

- What are the main tasks they complete or manage each day?

- Do they spend time in meetings, on the computer, working on a specific tangible deliverable, a combination of these?
- What computer software or tangible tools do they use?
- What are the biggest challenges they face each day and in general?
- What is their favorite part of their job and why?
- Any other questions about the person's day-to-day work will likely be beneficial for you to know

During this process, making connections to your own background will become natural and habitual, even if you don't realize it... which we will discuss in Pit Stop #2- Sharpening Your Story.

△△△

Lather, rinse, and repeat... by repeating the above steps, you will quickly solidify your network, you will learn more about the specific job you want (as well as which jobs you do not want), you will further realize the skills, experiences, and strengths that you could bring to the table, and you will build relationships with people who can influence the probability that you get hired. I provide further detail about the importance of the networking process below.

NETWORKING STARTS
BETWEEN TWO PEOPLE

Getting a job means being hired by another person who is employed by a company that also employs other people.

As strange as the above sentence sounds, it clearly identifies the fundamental process that every single job seeker has to go through in order to get hired. To get hired, you will have to communicate with people. Any other requirements a job seeker comes across during their job search were created by people. These same requirements can be adjusted, or even deleted, by people. Somewhere in the midst of all of the organized career fairs, recruiting websites, and collegiate corporate partnerships, a potential employer is talking to a potential employee about a job. All of this infrastructure that colleges, companies, and recruiting companies have created to transition job seekers to the job market can be helpful. However, for many people, it has the opposite effect. This infrastructure of career fairs and recruiting can serve as discouraging noise that distracts from the simple process of obtaining a job.

Rather than thinking about all of the ways to meet and build relationships with potential hirers, some students just hear "your GPA is too low" or "we are only interested in finance majors." This discouraging noise is misleading and distracting. Others might notice the sheer number of motivated individuals trying to obtain a job at these career fairs, which also can distract one from focusing on his or her own job search process. While the tools and infrastructure that universities and other companies create to facilitate the two-sided job seeking/employee seeking process are undoubtedly useful and beneficial to those who use them, there are many ways to obtain your dream job outside of these tools and infrastructure.

A potential hirer is just like you and me. They want to be around kind, hard-working, intelligent people who have fun and make money. Despite all the networking events, career websites, and competitive atmospheres that universities or career sites create, the simple conversation with a recruiter or hiring manager, which can occur anywhere at any time, is at the very core of the job search process. Don't talk yourself out of a career before you even understand how it relates to your own background, interests, and skills. Remember, just like a friend or Airbnb host has to be willing to host you, an employer has to be willing to hire you.

STARTING TO APPLY YOUR BACKGROUND

How do you know that you even want the job you are trying to get? You have likely observed someone who has experienced the job or who has knowledge of what the job entails. Your observations might have come from reading about it, watching a video, talking to someone who works closely with the specific role you are interested in, or even talking to someone who has that job themselves. If so, great. This observation exercise likely helped you further determine whether or not you like the idea of the job.

However, if you cannot pin point any specific observations that support your reasoning for wanting the job, then you probably don't even want the job or, at the very least, you are lagging behind other people who have worked to network with people who they can observe. Without networking, even if you know a job is your dream job, you are already behind candidates who are making relationships that enable them to draw comparisons between their experiences, background, and skills that they can bring to the table.

△△△

After practicing, understanding, and implementing the Road Map for this Pit Stop, you will:

- Recognize substantial networking opportunity
- Build numerous true relationships with people who could potentially connect you to your job
- Learn about many roles of potential interest
- Relate your background to those roles and the backgrounds of the people who will hire you
- Show interest and desire to learn about the role, giving you a leg up on any other candidates your potential hirer might come across

LOOKING BACK AT MY HOST EXPERIENCE

Here is how I learned the value of networking and obtained an awesome internship despite my low GPA at the time.

My sophomore year of my undergraduate studies, I built a true relationship with Shawn, who essentially hired me for my first internship. One year before that, I had a 2.64 GPA, and I was just starting to scan the internet and university career resources for a potential first internship. In looking through the available opportunities, I found very few listings for which I was "qualified", at least according to the minimum qualifications on the job postings. The jobs for which I was "qualified" did not appeal to me for various reasons including company reputations, compensation, location, and often the job itself. This was a very discouraging time. I felt that I had worked way too hard to have an average or below average start to my career, and I knew that I was much smarter than the job postings implied. In a desperate and worried state, I began to network using the university resources, specifically career fairs.

For a solid year before my first internship, I consistently handed my résumé to recruiters, class guest speakers, and career fairs, and I hoped they would get in touch with me. I would make small talk and try to sell myself and talk about my background rather than ask about what they do, what role they were hiring for, and drawing similarities between my own experience and skillset. Unknowingly, I was having a very one-sided, non-interactive conversation with each of these potential hirers, leaving little to no room to build a working relationship with them. Additionally, I usually didn't even have a firm understanding of what they did or what they were looking for me to do, and I wasn't asking the right questions to find out.

Luckily, I met a guy named Shawn on the golf course, and I was not at all thinking about the fact that he might be able to hire me. I was only playing golf, which had been engrained in my day-to-day activity for a long time. I simply got to know him by asking a few basic questions to avoid prolonged silence. I asked a few questions about what he did. To fill the time between golf shots and out of pure curiosity, I asked follow-up questions about things such as what the challenges were in that job, asking what he did in college, and asking him other relatively routine questions that I'd ask any new person on the golf course to fill the time.

Through this conversation, Shawn could tell

that I was simply interested in learning about his background and professional experience, but probably wasn't even thinking he'd hire me himself. This initial introductory conversation had already catalyzed my learning process about Shawn, and the conversation at the very least showed Shawn that I was willing to learn. Through further conversations on the golf course and even at lunch after the round, I was able to draw similarities between my education, background, and hobbies with his experience. In this manner, and without even realizing it at the time, I built a true relationship with Shawn. This certainly gave me a huge advantage when I expressed interest in working at his company in a role such as the ones in his department. When I applied for the internship, Shawn already knew me well and could see my willingness to learn, and I knew that I had already gained enough information to understand that I liked the idea of the job and how my experiences applied to it. As a result of this connection, the interview process was much less intimidating from my perspective, and I had already experienced what could be considered a prolonged informal interview in the sense that I had learned about him and the role and he had learned about me and my background. I received an internship offer soon after expressing interest and interviewing. Shawn knew of availability under a manager in his group, and recommended that I apply.

I had never even considered that networking

opportunities like this were available in my normal day-to-day activity, and I began to think about various friends I had with parents who would have been great additions to my network, as well as the many other opportunities that I was blind to. Fortunately, I fell into a situation where I networked with someone who ended up giving me a dream opportunity.

△△△

Now consider if you build 5-10 of these true relationships with older professionals that have the ability to hire. Your chances of getting a job that you are interested in is substantial. Keep in mind that you might even build relationships, and through that process learn that you don't really like the idea of what they do... that is great! This helps you learn about yourself, which will benefit in Pit Stop #2- Sharpening Your Story.

TIPS AND INSPIRATION FROM A ROAD TRIPPER

MAIN TAKEAWAYS

- Recognize your daily opportunity to build a network
- Try several platforms and atmospheres to network
- Stick to what's comfortable, and begin building those relationships
- Strength in numbers... you want to simply expose yourself to as much learning as possible with different professionals or people of the relevant industry

I was very lucky. You want as many "Shawns" as possible in your life to increase your odds of finding a job that interests you and also to increase your odds of being hired for one.

ΔΔΔ

Other Notes and Tips:

You can use any casual setting as an environment to build a network. Recognize that any setting is fair game. Each and every one of us spends our time doing something... we all have casual settings that we can utilize to build relationships. With that said, ALL settings are useful, so use the listed settings or come up with other settings as you see fit.

Without even recognizing it at the time, I was lucky enough to get to talk to a professional about his background and ask all the questions I wanted, even drawing comparisons of his background to mine. In hindsight, anyone can create this opportunity for themselves... often in their everyday lives.

You know yourself. You know you try your best to succeed, or, if you haven't, you have learned from your choices and want to succeed going forward. All you have to do is be yourself to SHOW people you are that good person who wants to succeed. If you do this long enough, you will find the job you want.

PIT STOP #2: SHARPENING YOUR STORY

Preparing for the Weather at Your Destination

SHARPENING YOUR STORY

*IN ORDER TO PREPARE FOR YOUR CHOSEN DES-
TINATION, YOU HAVE TO LOOK THROUGH YOUR
CLOSET TO SEE WHAT YOU CAN BRING WITH YOU*

We will now dive into Pit Stop #2-
Sharpening Your Story. Sharpening
Your Story is the creative process of reflecting on your background in detail in order to
understand your strengths and their application
to a job and to understand your weaknesses along
with your short-term, medium-term, and long-
term plans to overcome them. Throughout this Pit
Stop, you will iteratively relate your learnings from
Pit Stop #1 to your own story, enabling yourself to
focus your story on the most prominent points.

KNOW YOUR PAST SO YOU CAN USE IT IN THE FUTURE

When you are preparing for your road trip destination, you consider all of the things you know about the destination. As mentioned in Pit Stop #1, you consider factors such as the weather, the day-to-day activities, the type of nightlife and restaurants, and more. You want to pack items and fine tune yourself so that you are prepared to enjoy the destination while you are there. Similarly, in order to prepare for your dream job, you need to look at what you can bring with you. Just because your friend lives in a vacation spot doesn't mean they have room to host you. They might want to host a friend who has shown that they can bring something of value to the vacation spot. Your potential host will want to be sure you will be respectful of their home and that you are bringing things with you to safely enjoy the destination and also make it fun or beneficial to them.

Similarly, a hiring manager will want you to bring the skills or experiences **necessary** to accomplish the required tasks on the job so that there is mutual benefit from hiring you.

△△△

While reflecting on your past, you need to identify the skills and experiences that you can use to best grab the hiring manager's attention. This Pit Stop will teach you a variety of ways to identify your strengths and to improve your weaknesses.

ROAD MAP TO SHARPENING YOUR STORY

So how are you going to know what skills you can bring to the table?

$$\triangle\triangle\triangle$$

With your ideal job in mind:

1) Reflect on your background

1a) Schedule a block of time (1-3 hours) each day to sit and complete various exercises to reflect on yourself and your background

Do your best to schedule this time during a period where you will have some energy. Don't schedule it during a time where you will be mentally exhausted (for example, if you have a full day of class, do it before class).

1b) Ask yourself questions such as:

- What school projects or other projects throughout my life have been most enjoyable?
- What are my biggest accomplishments to date?

- What are my biggest failures to date?

Think through the experience of each accomplishment and failure and take notes.

1c) After you have completed at least a session of your own reflection with the steps above, take a free, simple personality quiz

Reputable quizzes at the very least provide a full spectrum of the typical behavior observed from people who chose the same responses. My favorite personality quiz can be found at www.16personalities.com.

△△△

During this time, you should solely focus on yourself, not any job description or anyone else. By creating an exhaustive list of all of your memorable past experiences and assessing where you have succeeded versus where you have not, you are cutting your metaphorical block of ice, which you can start sharpening into a masterpiece for your potential hirer.

2) After you have reflected on your past, identify and focus on your key strengths and weaknesses

Some helpful questions to ask yourself:

- Which strengths and weaknesses have the most significance in my current life and future goals?

Why? What make these strengths and weaknesses so important today?

- Can I explain each strength with an example? Tying strengths and weaknesses to specific events or a group of events helps make them tangible and helps you recognize the actions you took leading up to your successes and failures so that you can learn from them.

- Do you have a plan in process to mitigate your weaknesses? For example, if your weakness is public speaking, are you reading a book or taking a class to practice and improve?

- In what creative ways could you take immediate action to improve? Reference the trick laid out in the Tips and Inspiration section of this Pit Stop.

$$\triangle\triangle\triangle$$

Lather, rinse, repeat.... by making this Pit Stop a habit you will quickly identify the most relevant strengths, weaknesses, skills, and experiences from your background, meaning you will know what you should pack for your destination!

KNOWING YOURSELF REQUIRES SELF-REFLECTION

If you show up to the airport without identification, or without a ticket reflecting your destination, you won't get through security. Similarly, if you don't know your key strengths, your plan to attack your weaknesses, and your most relevant experiences and skills, you are not prepared to pass a recruiter's screening to even get your application in front of your potential hirer. Sharpening your story is necessary to fully understand your strengths and weaknesses and their relationship to your ideal job.

If you don't understand how you can take your memorable experiences and your previously developed skills and apply them to the job, you won't be able to put together an intriguing résumé or grab the attention of your potential hirer. Truly understanding your background and experience will enable you to dial in your résumé, portfolio, or website to a job description, which is the next Pit Stop on our Road Map to Your Job.

△△△

After practicing, understanding, and implementing the Road Map for this Pit Stop, you will:

- Recognize your biggest weakness
- Understand the power of your strengths and experiences
- Recognize basic skills that you do have or can quickly learn to display to potential hirers
- Recognize how you have learned or will learn from the weaknesses you have identified
- Accept your past failures and weaknesses as opportunities to exhibit your strengths

LOOKING BACK AT SHARPENING MY STORY

Let me tell you my experience in sharpening my story and where it led me:

After reflecting on my background and experiences, my personality, my desired career path, and the obstacles I had faced, I began to visualize how I could use the strengths and experiences that I did have in order to overcome those obstacles and move forward on my desired path. After thinking long and hard about my strengths and weaknesses, I knew the obvious weaknesses that would be a big hurdle for me: I had a low GPA, and I wanted a job in a different field than my exact studies.

During my day-to-day self-reflection, I came up with a plan to tackle these issues without omitting or ignoring them. If you have been a subscriber to my website, you may have already heard this story, but its value is worth reviewing it again here.

I took my low, but improving GPA from each semester and plotted them on a simple line plot to show my improvement (you really only need 3 semesters to show a decent trend).

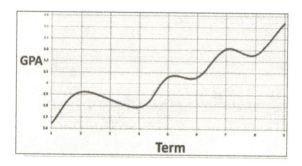

- I attached it to applications along with my résumé
- I printed the plot out and brought it to interviews

Not only did this turn my résumé weakness (low GPA) into a strength by showing that I learn from mistakes and quickly apply my learnings to improve, but it also required application of a skill relevant to my desired job, a simple trend analysis, which was also perfect for interview discussion.

To summarize, by sharpening my story, I was able to creatively grab the attention of recruiters despite my low GPA and lack of experience, obtain interviews at many companies throughout college, and obtain four offers for employment after graduation. I did all of this without actually progressing on my weaknesses immediately- I instead showed how I was already progressing and how I planned to continue. I would have never been able to do so without sharpening my story. We all work on our weaknesses anyway, and we are usually our biggest critic...so you just have to show how you are working on them.

TIPS AND INSPIRATION FROM A ROAD TRIPPER

MAIN TAKEAWAYS

Apply this Trick:

1) Get to know your weakness(es) for that job you want (you probably already know them)

Below are some questions to start with:

- What are the questions that you will struggle with in an interview?
- What are the things you want to hide on your application/résumé?

2) Creatively attack your weakness and make the potential hirer forget that weakness

2a) Find a blog or article about attacking the weakness and read a few paragraphs/posts

At the very least when questioned about a weakness you can intelligently respond with a blog or articles that you have read out of desire to improve. You don't have to overcome the weakness for the interview- just turn the weakness into a strength for the purpose of a résumé or interview. Show the potential hirer that the weakness is under attack.

While this process strongly depends on the weakness you are trying to overcome, you can find a mechanism to minimize or completely remove the chance of the potential hirer worrying about that weakness with a few simple steps.

2b) *If questioned about a weakness, acknowledge that you have a weakness*

Ignoring or lying about your weaknesses won't help anyone. Acknowledge it, and then research and make plans to overcome the weakness.

2c) *Study solutions to your weaknesses using the internet or other resources such as books, peers, and professors*

2d) *Use your relevant strengths to show the potential hirer you are attacking the weakness and seeing positive results*

3) Attack the weakness all the way through the interview

Since you identified this weakness for the interview... it likely is something you will want to work on anyway for the sake of your career.

After the interview, continue to mitigate this weakness using the path you set forth in preparation for the interview. This will only further prepare you for the job or next interview.

△△△

Other Notes and Tips:

Coffee can bring out some creative energy and enable you to reminisce on different events than you normally would. With that said, I definitely would not recommend using coffee often or at all if you already feel refreshed.

PIT STOP #3: POPULATING YOUR PLATFORM

WEBSITE, RÉSUMÉ, PORTFOLIO

Grabbing Your Host's Attention

POPULATING YOUR PLATFORM (WEBSITE, RÉSUMÉ, PORTFOLIO)

FOR YOUR HOST TO AGREE TO ACCOMMODATE YOU, YOU NEED TO GRAB THEIR ATTENTION AND SHOW THEM THAT YOUR BAG IS PACKED WITH THE THINGS THEY LOOK FOR IN A GUEST

Welcome to Pit Stop # 3- Populating Your Platform- the process of taking all of your important past experiences, skill developments, learnings, and even your failures, and specifically and creatively displaying them to stand out during a potential hirer's review.

WOW THE APPLICANT REVIEWER TO STAND OUT EARLY

Applying for a job online is like sending a message to your friend who is a local Instagram celebrity and receives a ton of messages each day asking to visit them in their vacation home or their downtown hotspot. Just because you know them doesn't guarantee that they will even read your message or choose to respond to you instead of to one of their other friends or relatives. Similarly, there is no guarantee a recruiter or hiring manager reads or responds to your application when sifting through the hundreds or thousands of applications.

Applications can include many different platforms on which you present your background, experiences, and skillset. Here is a brief list of some possible platforms:

- Résumé
- Cover Letter
- Portfolio
- Website

- Any other format that you use to show your background, experiences, and skillset in a job application

ΔΔΔ

There are many ways to populate your platform in a way that stands out and grabs a potential hirer's attention so that you can build a relationship and then book your metaphorical destination at their company. We will cover these in this Pit Stop. If your physical/local network (as opposed to the global network social media platforms provide) either doesn't have interesting opportunities or if it isn't easy to stand out in that local network, this Pit Stop will help you find a way to stand out from anywhere.

ROAD MAP TO POPULATING YOUR PLATFORM

How are you going to grab your potential hirer's attention?

ΔΔΔ

1) Choose a platform(s) (most will likely benefit from a résumé and website)

Below I provide a list of possible platforms and some ways that you could use them.

<u>Résumé</u>

Résumés are usually required for most job applications, but there are many ways to be creative with your résumé. For Example:

- Providing a link on top of your résumé to a more interactive platform such as a website with a video can immediately expand the viewer's interest

- Depending on the job, formatting the résumé in a colorful or more digestible manner can also grab attention

Portfolio

A portfolio can be in a variety of formats:

- Consider tangible items such as a binder showing your work (using pictures or text), or even a handful of tangible displays of your work (example: a diorama that you made for work or school)

Website

A website is versatile because you can add text, pictures, and even a video of yourself talking about your relevant background. Besides finding creative ways to tell your story on the site, you can even:

- Find a website such as www.godaddy.com to search for and purchase a domain name

- Purchase a unique domain name for fairly cheap

- Choose a domain name that is relevant to the role of your interest

I named a website www.givemeajobatcompanyxyz.com to grab the recruiter's attention and obtain an interview (note: the company name was actually included in the domain name, but I replaced it with "companyxyz" in this example for privacy purposes). I provide more information regarding this exercise in the Looking Back at Populating My Platform section of this Pit Stop.

Youtube, KickStarter, Etc.

- If you have any existing videos for projects or work that you have done, or if you even want to create one for your application, this gives a potential hirer a chance to see and hear your enthusiasm

- Videos can often be embedded or linked on your website or résumé

<u>Social Media Applications</u>

- Snapchat Filters can even be used to say "HIRE ME" and grab a recruiter's attention at their very location

- Your LinkedIn, Instagram and other profiles can also be a great place to display your work

The list could be endless...be creative. More information is provided below in this Pit Stop to help.

ΔΔΔ

Always be creative when considering your desired platform(s). There is always a way to be unique and tie your background to a job in a way that pops out in comparison to all of the standard applications that a recruiter has to screen. Reference both the example and trick I provided in Pit Stop #2 (in the main takeaways section), as well as the example in this Pit Stop for ideas.

After you have chosen:

2) Conduct a daily ritual in populating each of your

chosen platforms

2a) Start by identifying the significant experiences that you have had relevant to the role (example questions below)

- What past project/experience examples can I work into my résumé?

- How can I creatively show or further explain these examples to someone?

- How can I grab someone's attention with one of these examples?

2b) Work your examples into a website, portfolio, or another format to creatively highlight your strengths and attack your weaknesses

Website builders make it is easy for anyone to create a nice looking website within 1-2 hours of time (FOR FREE!) Below find some examples of free or cheap website builders:

- www.weebly.com
- www.wix.com
- www.squarespace.com

Snapchat filters, Google Ads, and other platforms can also be potential creative outlets to grab a potential hirer's attention.

2c) Continue to work your résumé examples into your chosen platform until you feel good about it (get those strengths to pop off the page!)

Do you think grabbing a potential hirer's attention doesn't apply to your field?

Even if it isn't a game-changer for you to get hired, creatively populating a platform to display your relevant skills will, at the very least, strengthen your own knowledge of the content you want to focus on for growth or to show and explain in any interview (informal or formal).

$$\triangle \triangle \triangle$$

Getting into this daily ritual will not only allow you to build out your platform to communicate your skillset to anyone, but it will also make your job search and preparation more fun (and therefore more enjoyable and sustainable) while also building your confidence in your experiences, which we will discuss more in the next Pit Stop.

DISPLAYING PREPAREDNESS SHOWS COMMITMENT

Creatively populating a résumé, website, or other platform not only grabs the attention of your potential hirer, but also shows them that you took the time and committed yourself to presenting your story to them in a way that shows you understand its application to the job.

In order to grab their attention and give a succinct explanation of your background and its application to the job, you will likely have to "do your homework" and really understand the job as well as your own background and experiences. Therefore, creating a résumé, website or other platform that creatively shows your background and its application is a crucial, rewarding task on the road map to your job.

LOOKING BACK AT POPULATING MY PLATFORM

During the early part of my senior year of college, I accepted a full-time job offer for the same department that I had previously interned in San Diego, California. I enjoyed my remaining college days, and then, after graduation, I moved from the suburbs of Chicago to San Diego. I enjoyed my first full-time job, but I decided that I wanted to move back to Illinois to be closer to family and friends. To me, everything besides work seemed second hand without family and friends. I was afraid to ask my boss if I could transfer to the Illinois location, as I had only been there for 1 year, and I was appreciative for all he had taught me through his mentorship.

In the meantime (instead of looking to transfer within the same company), I looked at other external opportunities to move back. I saw a job opening at another large aerospace company and it was similar to my role at the time. Because I missed my home, I began to dig deep, and I thought back to when I was a student at the University of Illinois. As a student, this same company with the open role had invited me to attend an on-site interview, but I was unable to attend due to prior obligations. I asked to reschedule the interview for another time, but I never heard back to reschedule. I thought this was pretty unlucky. However, now that I was trying to move back to the Midwest, I took a peek at their openings. How was I supposed to get their attention though when they had all of these students ready to enter the job market from U of I and other great schools? I knew I had to get creative. During this process, I literally made a website called www.give-meajobatcompanyxyz.com (the company name was actually included in the domain name, but I replaced it with "companyxyz" in this example for privacy purposes). I used an easy website builder tool (Google Sites) to very cheaply build a simple website with a video of me expressing my interest, qualifications, and what made me fit for Company XYZ.

Google Site's website analytic tools showed me not only when someone viewed my site, but also the city from which they viewed my site. Fairly soon after I had applied, I saw that people from the exact location of the company were viewing my website. They emailed me, set up a phone interview, and due to my familiarity with my background and its application to the role, I received a job offer. Ultimately, I turned down the job offer as it still wasn't close enough to my family and friends (still a four hour drive). San Diego was a four hour flight.

With that said, the creativity and work that I put in to trying to get a job near home made me realize it was worth talking to my manager about a transfer. He encouraged me to wait a little longer before deciding, so I did (out of respect since he hired me). He then connected me with the hiring managers from our site in Illinois, and they were glad to facilitate my transfer.

Here is the moral of my story: if you want a job badly enough, you will truly enjoy creatively attacking the job description and you will figure out how to show your best strengths and the experiences from your past that make you qualified.

While I was preparing my résumé for internships and jobs during college, I would wake up and immediately enjoy a coffee, sit at my desk with my music playing, and dive into the creative process of exhibiting my skillset for potential job roles. I found a sense of reflection in building and dialing in my résumé and website because it helped me gain confidence and understand my strengths and how I could attack my weaknesses. Once I started getting creative and building graphs and websites to make my story stand out and more visual, I really began to have fun working on it.

△△△

Adapt the process I described to fit your schedule and interests, and make your application process fun.

TIPS AND INSPIRATION FROM A ROAD TRIPPER

MAIN TAKEAWAYS

Enjoy populating your platform.

Make the process an enjoyable part of your routine. If job prep isn't your thing, make it fun. Have a drink or snack while you build your website or write your résumé. Make it your daily ritual to go to the coffee shop and work on your résumé. However you do it, add some fun to your job search to allow yourself to power through the process.

This Pit Stop is not a guide for critiquing résumés or portfolios, but a guide of how to enjoy it and make it stand out. There are plenty of resources to help you critique your résumé. Simply Google "How to Edit Your Résumé" to find resources.

PIT STOP #4: BUILDING TRUE CONFIDENCE AND THE ABILITY TO SELL

*Convincing Your Host
to Accommodate You*

BUILDING TRUE CONFIDENCE AND THE ABILITY TO SELL

WHILE YOUR POTENTIAL HOST KNOWS YOU ARE PACKED AND INTERESTED IN THEIR VACATION DESTINATION, THEY WILL LIKELY HAVE QUESTIONS FOR YOU ABOUT YOUR PREPAREDNESS AND EXPECTATIONS

Welcome to Pit Stop #4- Building True Confidence and the Ability to Sell. In this Pit Stop we will work to funnel all of the work you have done so far to the front of your mind so that you can access it and verbalize it in the form of an intelligent response to anyone, anywhere, and at any time. You never know when you will run into the right connection, and you need to be able to confidently speak to them.

PRACTICE MAKES PERFECT

Telling your story as much as possible in different settings, with different visuals, and to as many people as possible will enable you to grow confident and fluent in telling your story.

Your popular friend is much more likely to host you at their vacation home if you can show and explain to them how you are prepared and what you expect from the experience. You have to be ready to explain this to them at any time.

Similarly, when you are communicating with someone whom you know could influence the likelihood that a company will hire you, you need to be versatile and use the conversation to your advantage. To do this, you have to listen carefully to them and also have your relevant skills available at the forefront of your mind. This will help you to intelligently guide them through your website, résumé, portfolio, or any other platform that you might use to explain how your background, experiences, and skill set are applicable to the job.

△△△

As you network and practice the exercises described in the previous Pit Stops, you will start to notice that things you learn during your network conversations can help you identify your relevant skills and experiences to highlight during your application process and the interview.

ROAD MAP TO BUILDING TRUE CONFIDENCE AND THE ABILITY TO SELL

How will you become fluent and confident in showing and explaining your backstory when it matters the most?

△△△

Repetitions and Variety. Simply practice telling your story to as many people as possible, in as many ways as possible, and answer all of their questions. I provide exercises for this Pit Stop below.

1) Create opportunities to explain your story

There are so many outlets you can use to talk about your background, experiences, and skill set and how they all apply to a job.

1a) Make a list of the settings that you could use to practice telling people your story (examples below)

- University Career Centers
- Friends

- Classmates
- Family Members
- Roommates
- Professors
- Advisors
- Teaching Assistants
- New people at Happy Hour
- University Career Fairs
- The list goes on and on....

1b) Set aside time to use some of the above resources to explain your résumé, website, portfolio, or whatever platform you plan to use or already used in your job application

The more you communicate your story (whether it be to the same person in many different ways, many people the same exact way, or somewhere in between), the better you will know it yourself.

△△△

Once you have set aside time with at least a few of the resources above, you have created opportunities to become more familiar with your background. The more time you have set aside, the more repetitions you will get to build your confidence in showing someone your background and its application to the job you want.

2) Stick to a simple storytelling method

2a) *In order to be consistent, logical, and confident, stick to a consistent method*

The "STAR" Method is quite popular at universities and is recommended for interview preparation. This method can be used when asked a question, or also when you just want to explain anything (such as an example from your background).

I provide a Star Method Definition and links to STAR Method examples in the appendix. Alternatively, you can simply Google "STAR interview method" to learn how it works.

Any consistent story-telling format is sufficient, as long it gives the listener:

- Context regarding the topic you are explaining
- A more detailed breakdown of the tasks you needed to complete
- An explanation of how you executed the tasks
- The result of your actions

$$\triangle\triangle\triangle$$

Using a consistent method enables you to break down any experience or story that you want to talk about in a logical way that is digestible for any listener. Since you will become very familiar with your examples as you are typically explaining them in the same exact way, it will become easy for you to tweak aspects of the story to emphasize important points depending on the question you are answering.

3) Use your résumé, website, portfolio or any other platform you might have available to explain your background

Your platform will be more memorable than your story alone. All of the preparation you did in Pit Stop #3 was to give you a more fluent, tangible start to building your confidence, but is also important when presenting your story in person.

ΔΔΔ

Using visual or creative ways to tell your story will only help you learn it better because you have visual or other associations allowing you to easily recall important points you want to use.

4) Be open and respond to all questions

4a) Encourage questions, and answer all of them thoroughly

Be sure to tell your listener to ask any questions they might have. Even answer basic questions in detail. The more thorough you are in answering questions, the more familiar you will become with the fundamentals of your background and how they apply to the fundamentals of the role you want.

5) Research the company and role

While you have already learned about the company and role through networking and populating your platform, there are likely basic company facts, competitor information, parts of the job description, and relevant industry news that you aren't quite familiar with. The company's website as well as websites like "Glassdoor" and "Indeed" will have basic information available to learn about the company.

5a) Ask yourself questions like:

- What products do they make?
- What industry are they in?
- Who are their main competitors?
- Who would I be working for in this role?
- Who is the CEO?
- What will be the daily tasks required from me in this role?
- What skills are most important to the potential hirer?
- What industry language might I use in this role?
- What news outlets publish information about this industry?

YOUR CONFIDENCE =
THEIR CONFIDENCE

Networking can occur in so many different scenarios, times, and places, and therefore you need to be confident and ready when an opportunity presents itself... which could be any time! You can't waste time or miss opportunities because you are afraid or because you are unsure of how you can confidently show how your background is applicable to the opportunity.

Building confidence to tell your story prepares you for any variation of a question, from any audience, in any setting. Use the sources described throughout this Pit Stop as well as any others you can think of to practice telling your story, and do it as much as you can until you know how to tell your story inside and out.

Consider this:

Your relatively new friend's parents told him or her that they can take five friends to their tropical beach house for spring break. The boat at the beach house fits a maximum of 6 people, and your friend already invited four others. Your friend mentions that he or she is concerned because although one of the people going on the trip has a boating license, none of them have ever put a boat into the water. Whether your friend knows it or not, he or she is opening the door for you or someone else to show them why it'd be beneficial for them to host a guest for Spring Break. If you are interested in potentially staying at their nice vacation destination, likely FOR FREE, you had better be ready to sell your friend on the good, fun, safe times that you would have together if they hosted you. When they ask, they don't want a hesitant answer... which is likely all they are expecting if they are expecting any response at all.

If you give them a response like, "That'd be a buzzkill if you couldn't even get out on the water" they will almost certainly end up hosting someone else instead during Spring Break. However, you could excuse yourself from your friend for five or ten minutes and watch a couple of YouTube videos on how to put a boat in the water. Then you could come back to your friend and say something like, "I've actually watched a few instructional videos on putting a boat in the water and my uncle also has a boat, so I can call him and ask him to walk us through it."

$$\triangle\triangle\triangle$$

This positive answer is much more helpful

and forward looking than the latter, showing your friend he or she needs you, and it definitely plants a seed for your potential trip. Perhaps you've even helped someone put a boat in the water a few times and could mention that. Whatever you can do to describe your potential contribution to mitigate your friend's concern without lying to them will increase your chances of going on the trip.

LOOKING BACK AT BUILDING CONFIDENCE

During the fall interview season of my senior year (after my first two summer internships) as an undergraduate student, I obtained three job offers despite the challenges I faced relative to other applicants. Looking back at how I succeeded, I used to spend an hour a day studying my story, my strengths, my weaknesses, and how to explain their job application. To me, this was an easy way to get my mind going in the morning and wake up before heading to the gym, so the hour I spent on this task each morning felt like no time at all. The fall semester had a lot of career fairs and guest speakers in class that enabled face time with recruiters and potential hiring managers from many companies, so I really just got in this routine to be fresh for the possible conversations I might have each day.

I often would sit at my desk before heading to the gym, drink a coffee or a pre-workout drink, and in some cases I would even talk out loud explaining my résumé, my website, or just answering interview-type questions to myself. I really didn't realize how helpful this activity was at the time.

I merely found it fun to creatively put together my résumé and job applications, and I hoped that I could somehow stand out amongst my peers. Routinely asking myself these questions and going through my story in my head was a strong foundation for the confidence I built even before the interview process, which is probably why companies invited me to interview in the first place. Knowing that recruiters/job sites would receive hundreds of "qualified" applicants drove me to get really creative and fluent with my story to ensure that I would stand out, and it also ended up making my interview preparation easy.

Beyond my normal routine, I would sit down and casually talk to my roommates about my job applications, résumé, website, and my background in general which empowered them to ask me a variety of questions (my roommates were going through the same process, and they were smart, so they definitely asked great questions.) Once I started to get interview invites, I even set aside time with my sister to conduct a few formal mock interviews. I provide more information on mock interviews in Pit Stop #5.

Over time I have realized that the actions I mentioned above:

1) Made me absolutely fluent with my story and how I could explain my value to a recruiter or hirer, regardless of the atmosphere or questions they

asked

2) Built up my comfort in using creative and visual tools to facilitate the intriguing explanation of my background, experiences, and skills and their direct application to a job

△△△

Repetitions and variety results in fluency and also even generates some new ideas and excitement that enhance your explanation of your story. Not only will this Pit Stop prepare you for a career fair or day-to-day networking, but it also will prepare you for an informal talk with a recruiter, a phone-screen with a recruiter or hiring manager, and it will make your formal interview preparation much easier and less daunting.

TIPS AND INSPIRATION FROM A ROAD TRIPPER

MAIN TAKEAWAYS

Be thorough in responding to even the simplest questions about the role or your background. This will allow you to become comfortable explaining to anyone how your past and present experiences and how your skillset applies to the job. Having a thorough understanding of even the simplest questions is the foundation for your comfort.

Takeaway:

You build your confidence in this phase because an interview isn't always in a formal setting, it really could be anywhere (at a networking event, on the golf course, at a school club event, etc.)

Looking up websites of the company, competitors, the job description, and industry news will simply remind you of your goal and allow you to continue to trace it back to your story mentally, enabling you to form the connection into sentences.

PIT STOP #5: RUNNING OVER THE INTERVIEW

Confirming Your Destination

RUNNING OVER THE INTERVIEW

YOU HAVE TO REVIEW YOUR ITINERARY AND SOME-
TIMES ADD SOME LAST MINUTE DETAILS BEFORE
YOU CAN SUBMIT YOUR RESERVATION REQUEST
AND RECEIVE YOUR BOOKING CONFIRMATION

Here in Pit Stop #5, we will learn the process of Running over the Interview- preparing to answer any question with your powerful, dialed in background. This Pit Stop will provide a framework and tools for you to complete your story/response preparation, refresh some fundamentals, and calm your mind before interview day.

REVIEW YOUR PREVIOUS PIT STOPS TO BE FRESH

Consider the example mentioned in Pit Stop # 4 about your friend's beach house boat. Your friend knows you are interested and noticed something in your early discussions or messages that made them interested in further discussion with you. You will want to be prepared to respond to any clarifying questions your friend might have about your background and expectation for the trip. Your friend might want to know what kind of boat you helped your uncle put into the water. While you might not have put the same kind of boat in the water that your friend needs help with, you can certainly explain the similarities and other resources that you know can help you get their kind of boat into the water.

Similarly, an interview is simply the conversation in which you can respond to clarifying questions from your potential hirer or even refresh them on the specific experiences or skills that you know you can apply to the job. This conversation is where they decide to give you the job, if they haven't already decided to give it to you. Just like you have to review your itinerary and sometimes add last minute details, interviews are necessary for the hirer/recruiter to make sure that they see a mutual benefit in hiring.

$$\triangle\triangle\triangle$$

You likely have been looking at more than one opportunity, so now is the time to take all of your preparation from the previous Pit Stops and dial it towards the job for which you have an interview.

ROAD MAP TO RUNNING OVER YOUR INTERVIEW

So, how are you going to prepare to crush your interview?

$$\triangle\triangle\triangle$$

1) Prepare for the interview day

1a) Review several interview questions and practice responses by yourself

In a sense, this practice is very similar to the exercises described in Pit Stop #4, only instead of flat-out explaining your background to yourself or others, you are rehearsing your responses to specific potential interview questions about your background.

Rehearsing these alone to start gives you the chance to refresh a lot of the key points you became familiar with in Pit Stop #4 and also gives you the chance to practice tweaking the way you explain an example to address specific questions (if even necessary).

Find common interview questions in the appendix.

△△△

You can simply read these questions to yourself and think about your response, or you can respond by actually talking out loud if you feel comfortable doing that.

2) Diversify your practice

2a) To diversify your practice, common interview questions to practice with can be found in many ways:

- Google "Common Interview Questions"

- Look at websites such as "Glassdoor" or "Indeed" and review the interview questions available on their sites

- Often you can find interview questions used at the specific company and sometimes even for the exact role of your interest

- Visit the career center on your campus or their website, which often provides lists of common interview questions, sometimes even for specific jobs

- Read books regarding Interview Preparation

- Many other ways

Most interviews involve at least a few behavioral

interview questions, which are typically more general and not job specific.

Interviewers use behavioral questions to learn how you behave or respond to different scenarios. These can be rehearsed and usually re-used in interviews for other roles if necessary.

2b) *Google "Common Behavioral Interview Questions and Responses" to find good practice material or reference some good examples in the appendix of this book*

$$\triangle \triangle \triangle$$

Once you have gotten familiar with some common interview questions and how you can respond to them with the examples and storytelling method you became familiar with in Pit Stop #4, you are ready to practice a formal interview.

3) Conduct a mock interview with a friend or at a career center

Career centers definitely can help you with this, but often your friends or classmates who are seeking similar jobs actually know more about the role and can ask more realistic interview questions. If you setup mock interviews with friends or relatives, make sure they know you need them to take it seriously.

Alternatively, and to be more formal in your preparation, career centers or other professionals can schedule a mock interview with you.

3a) Be sure to set guidelines for the amount of time, types of questions asked, and any other variables that you can identify for your mock interview

3b) Prepare for the mock interview and dress in similar or the same clothing you plan to wear to the real interview if possible

Keeping the variables and even minute details such as the clothing you wear consistent with your expectation for the real interview will allow you to take advantage of "state dependent learning" and simply feel more comfortable interviewing in your attire.

Getting comfortable with dressing up to do a formal mock interview (these can be daunting if you aren't confident with your answers) usually ends up being more difficult than getting comfortable for the real interview since you are less practiced.

ΔΔΔ

After completing a couple mock interviews, there is not much else you can do to rehearse for the real thing. Continue to do mock interviews if you have available time and if you still feel discomfort. The last few steps in this Pit Stop will help you settle, handle your nerves, and give you a peace of mind for the actual interview.

4) Research, Research, Research

4a) *Prepare for potential questions, topics, and determine what you want to know from the interviewer*

What will the employer likely ask in the interview?

As stated previously, websites like "Glassdoor", "Indeed," and several others have interview questions by company and role. Reviewing these questions can never hurt, repetitions only help.

Questions that are job specific are often geared directly towards the job descriptions, so review it to see what they might ask.

What questions do you have for the interviewer? Asking about the challenges the hiring manager faces for that role can set you up to show that you can help.

4b) *Follow your normal routine the day of your interview*

- Stay consistent with your practicing habits the day-of

If you typically wake up, have coffee, and then practice, do the same thing on interview day.

- Remember the interview is literally a conversation

If you have worked through the first four Pit Stops, you have already done the prep.

- List questions that you still have and keep the list with

you for the interview

Interviews are a two-way street so be sure to ask questions that help you feel certain that the role is for you. Everyone feels nervous, but all you have to do is breathe, remember to take your time, and talk to the interviewer just like you did in any conversation you had during your preparation.

If you start to get really nervous, tell yourself inside to take your time and slow down. If you focus on that thought alone, your mind won't be able to sustain your nervousness for long.

- Review your strengths and weaknesses

Since these are at the core of any example or experience you discuss during the interview, refreshing yourself on these will keep them fresh for your interview.

DIAL-IN YOUR PLATFORM AND CONFIDENCE FOR THE INTERVIEW

Now that you have the interview, this Pit Stop enables you to take your platform, stories and examples, confidence, and all of your other preparation and dust it off to focus it on the role for which you are interviewing. Preparing for the interview will not only give you a peace of mind beforehand, but it will also greatly increase your chances of receiving a job offer. While you have done a lot of preparation prior to this Pit Stop, it is quite important that you refresh yourself on your stories and examples in order to focus them on this role in particular.

You might have been looking at other roles, and this Pit Stop is necessary for you to focus your platform, stories, and examples on the specific role for which you are interviewing. Explaining your platform and background in a general way is often well-received and sometimes might even get you a job offer. However, explaining your background in general and then specifically highlighting the most relevant information to the role for which you are interviewing can greatly increase your chances at receiving a job offer. The interviewer will notice and appreciate your specificity, especially when you are interviewing for more competitive jobs.

△△△

You are likely a very busy person. Universities often have pretty challenging schedules for their students, and you likely have other goals as well. Preparing for your interview can minimize stress and optimize your performance in school because you will be happier, have less to worry about, feel more confident, and you will likely sleep better.

LOOKING BACK AT MY INTERVIEWS

Thinking back, when I had successfully completed Pit Stop #4 and repetitively practiced telling my story in a variety of ways to become fluent and confident in explaining my background, I slept better. As I began to prepare for interviews, I quickly noticed that my fluency in explaining my story was very easy to translate into responses to specific interview questions. The tremendous confidence, versatility, interview performance, peace of mind, and simple plan all make interview day almost enjoyable.

When I began receiving interview invitations, I knew that all I needed to do was practice a little bit more to become comfortable with a formal interview for the specific company and role. My morning routine remained the same except instead of spending some of that time explaining my story and its application to a job to others, I spent that time taking those examples and skills I had used in my explanation to others and tweaked them into the form of a response to specific interview questions.

This minor adjustment came fairly easy, and consistently practicing some interview questions and conducting a few formal mock interviews enabled me to succeed in many interviews.

ΔΔΔ

After interview season my senior year of undergraduate, I received 3 job offers, all of which I could have seen myself happily accepting. To conclude my senior year, I decided to accept the job offer at the same company I had interned for two summers.

TIPS AND INSPIRATION FROM A ROAD TRIPPER

MAIN TAKEAWAYS

Make a Snapchat filter for your interview that says "Hire <Your Name>."

You can easily create something creative such as a snapchat filter to grab attention, and these creative tricks can be an easy way to break the ice.

TIME FOR YOU TO TAKE YOUR ROAD TRIP

It's your turn. While I luckily built a network that led me to a young professional career that crushed my own expectations, you can apply my learnings to take control of your career.

Start networking. Call up that Uber or Lyft to go to your next club meeting, happy hour or other activity and make sure to talk to people. The more you network, the easier and more fun it becomes, and the better your chances are of obtaining your dream job. Don't stop there.

Reflect on your background. While networking is very important, spend time away from friends, social media, and all other distractions. Be selfish and actually think about your story, who you are, and what things you have done. If you HAVE to be on that new iPhone or laptop, go to www.16personalities.com or a similar site and use some time to reflect on YOU. The better you understand your own background and habits, the better you can explain to someone how you are going to tackle job tasks. Keep working on yourself.

Get creative and display your relevant background in a fun, interesting way. Once you have a grasp on your background, taking the important parts and creatively presenting them on a résumé, website, or other platform is easy and fun. With today's technology, there are so many different ways to make your application pop out at a recruiter or potential hirer. Get your creative juices flowing and make it happen. Get ready to explain your masterpiece.

Practice explaining your background to anyone, everyone, and their friends. Explain it as much as possible. The more you explain your story, and in the more *ways* you explain your story, the easier and more fun it will become. In the end, listeners will see you as the CEO of yourself and your future. You will have their attention. With that said, be sure to close the deal.

To close the deal, refresh yourself for interviews and relax. Make sure you feel comfortable with the most important information you want to share. Then, stick to your routine and focus on relaxing and taking care of yourself. When the time comes, go do your best and don't look back.

Find the job that will take you where you want to go. Perhaps you will earn a free graduate degree, learn something valuable to others, or meet a person who inspires you to give back.

I hope you enjoyed the Road Map to Your Job. Thank you for reading.

APPENDIX
Definitions, Links, and References

DEFINITIONS

PIT STOP DEFINITIONS, STAR METHOD DEFINITION, OTHER DEFINITIONS

I provide definitions and references/ tools below. Reference these as needed during your reading and exercises.

△△△

PIT STOP DEFINITIONS

Pit Stop #1- Building Your Sound Network

Building Your Sound Network: is the process of getting to truly know people, what they do, what their skills and challenges are, and relating your background to their daily lives.

Pit Stop #2- Sharpening Your Story

Sharpening Your Story: is the creative process of reflecting on your background in detail to understand your strengths and their application to a job and to understand your weaknesses along with your short-term, medium-term, and long-term plans to overcome them.

Pit Stop # 3- Populating Your Platform

Populating Your Platform: is the process of taking all of your important past experiences, skill developments, learnings, and even your failures, and specifically and creatively displaying them to stand out during a potential hirer's review.

Pit Stop #4- Building True Confidence and the Ability to Sell

Building True Confidence and the Ability to Sell: is the process in which you'll work to funnel all of the work you have done so far to the front of your mind so that you can access it and verbalize it in the form of an intelligent response to anyone, anywhere, and at any time.

Pit Stop # 5- Running over the Interview

Running over the Interview: is the process of preparing to answer any question with your powerful, dialed in background.

STAR METHOD DEFINITION

Interviewers appreciate the situation, task, action, result (STAR) method because it enables them to understand and note all of the information that they might consider to be relevant to the job. Since interviewee's using the Star Method include four different segments of information in their responses to a question, the method also makes responses easier for the interviewer to digest.

I define each of the four segments of the Star Method below.

Situation: Describe a recent scenario, obstacle, or situation that you experienced.

Task: Describe the specific requirement(s), goal(s), and/or deliverables that you were asked to or that you decided to complete. If possible, specifically identify numbers, due dates, or other metrics that were important.

Action: Describe the specific exercises and/or activities that you worked through as well as the possible alternatives. Explain why you chose these activities and/or exercises as opposed to the other choices.

Results: Describe what happened as a result of your actions.

Specifically:

- What did you gain through your actions?

- How well did your actions meet the requirements, goals, and/or deliverables?

- What did you learn and what, if anything, might you do differently going forward?

While I provide links to Star Method examples later in this appendix, you can find more information regarding the Star Method and similar techniques by searching for "STAR Method" on Google or other websites.

OTHER MISCELLANEOUS DEFINITIONS

State Dependent Learning: is the phenomenon through which memory retrieval is most efficient when an individual is in the same state of consciousness as they were when the memory was formed.

Job: Any task, internship, career, or role that requires screening before you can do it. While I use the word "Job" throughout this book, the practices described in the book are applicable any time a person is trying to stand out to obtain a role or position.

Potential Hirer/ Hiring Manager: Any person influencing the likelihood that you receive an offer for a role or position. These people could be recruiters, actual managers of a department within a company, or any other person with influence on your ability to get a role or position. Throughout this book, I use the words "potential hirer" and "hiring manager" in an effort to cover the broad variety of people with influence on your job application process.

LINKS AND REFERENCES

HELPFUL WEBSITES, COMMON INTERVIEW QUESTIONS, STAR METHOD EXAMPLES

HELPFUL WEBSITES

Here is a list of helpful websites to use in general during your job application/ search process.

Websites to help you learn about yourself and present your story:

www.16personalities.com

www.weebly.com

www.squarespace.com

www.wix.com

www.godaddy.com

Websites to help you learn about a company, job, or a specific role and prepare for an interview:

www.glassdoor.com

www.indeed.com

COMMON INTERVIEW QUESTIONS

Below is a list of common interview questions and a few links to more. Please keep in mind that this list is not an all- inclusive and the more questions you practice the more prepared you will be for your interview.

- Tell me a little about yourself...

- Why do you want this job?

- Why should we hire you?

- What are your strengths?

- What are your weaknesses?

- Tell me about a time when you made a mistake...

- Tell me about a time when you had to deal with a conflict...

You can find more examples and recommended responses via Google search or at websites such as www.glassdoor.com, www.indeed.com, or www.themuse.com.

STAR METHOD EXAMPLES

Below I provide links to websites that provide STAR Method examples. There are many other websites and resources that you can use to find examples such as a University Career Center, job interview books (found in a library), or several other websites (found via Google).

https://www.thebalancecareers.com/what-is-the-star-interview-response-technique-2061629

https://theinterviewguys.com/star-method/

https://zety.com/blog/star-method-interview